Frog Cards

Catherine Baker

Explorer Challenge

What does this turn into?

OXFORD
UNIVERSITY PRESS

Contents

A Frog Card 4

A Fun Frog! 10

Lots of Fun Animals! 16

Paper Frogs 18

Look Back, Explorers 19

A Frog Card

1 Get all the things.

2

Fold the paper.

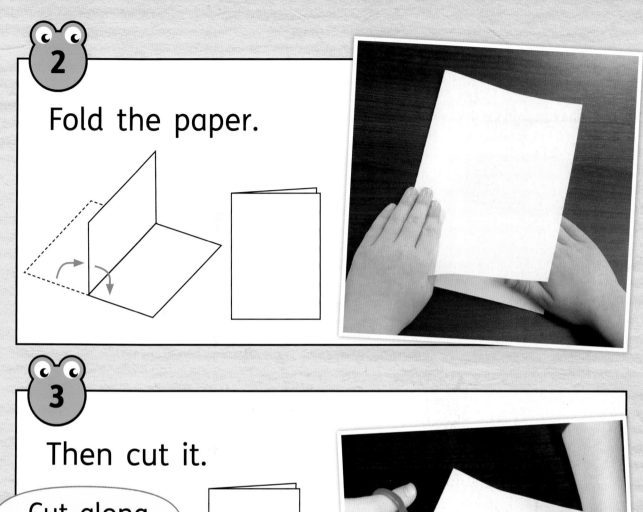

3

Then cut it.

Cut along this bit.

4

Fold the paper back at the cut.

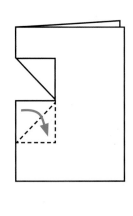

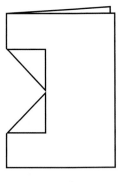

5

Unfold the bits.
Open up the paper.

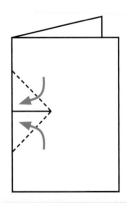

Fold in this bit.

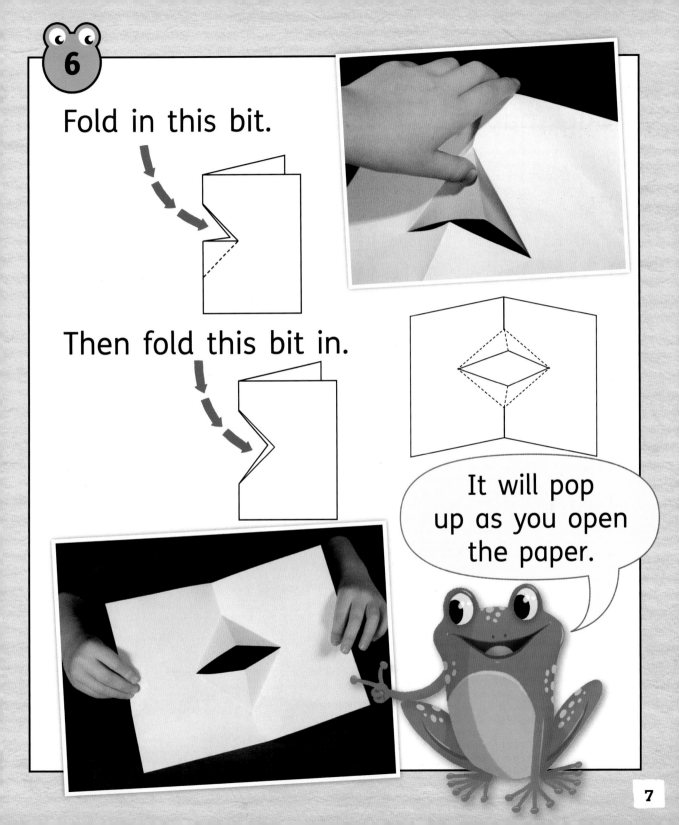

Then fold this bit in.

It will pop up as you open the paper.

7

Stick paper on the back of the
card.

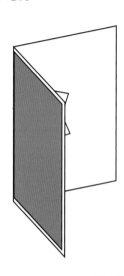

Add a frog with the pens.

It is a
frog card!

A Fun Frog!

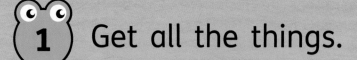 **1** Get all the things.

2 Add the pen.

3

Cut this paper and stick it on.

Stick it!

4

Fold it!

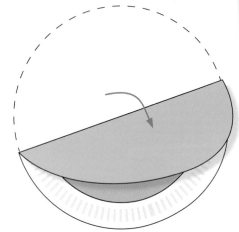

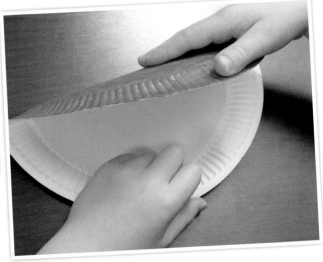

5

Cut the legs.

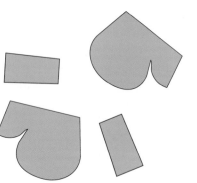

6

Stick the legs on the frog.

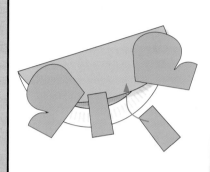

Add the legs.

7

Add dots with the pen.

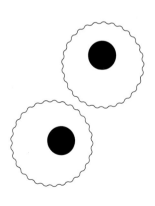

Stick on all the bits.

This is a fun frog!

Lots of Fun Animals!

frog

parrot

chicken

panda

fish

cat

fox

big fish

Paper Frogs

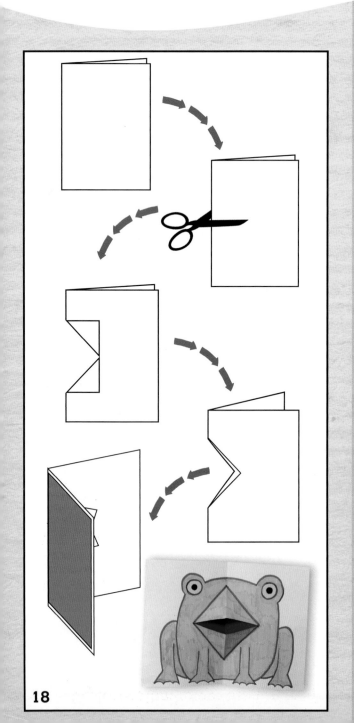

Look Back, Explorers

What is the first thing you should do to make a frog card?

How do you add dots on page 13?

What are the fun frog's eyes made of?

Did you find out what this turned into?

What's Next, Explorers?

Now read about Biff, Chip and Kipper making get-well cards for Gran …

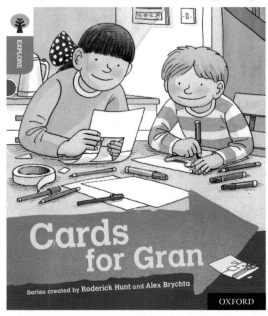

Explorer Challenge
for *Cards for Gran*

What does Mum make with this paper?